Cryptocurrency

Explaining The Rules And Making Sure Everyone Plays
By The Rules In The Wild World Of Cryptocurrency

*(The Complete Guide To Trading Cryptocurrencies: How
To Profit In Both Bull And Bear Markets)*

Dirk Oberndorfer

TABLE OF CONTENT

Introduction

Fundamental analysis and technical analysis have certain similarities, however fundamental analysis and technical analysis take quite distinct approaches. When assessing a stock, it is essential to have a solid understanding of each of these factors. Charts, market indicators, and several other tools are used by technical analysts in order to forecast future price changes.

They investigate the trends of supply and demand over a period of time, as well as the patterns of transaction volume on a certain stock or index.

On the other hand, fundamental analysts concentrate their attention on the financial data of companies as well as the economic information on the sectors in which the stocks trade (sometimes referred to as industries). They are interested with things like business earnings reports, profit margins, unemployment rates, and the growth rates of gross domestic product (GDP). They investigate these economic aspects to find out how the demand for and supply of a given item will change as a result of those factors.

Technical analysis focuses more on the price fluctuations of a stock or an index by analyzing previous records of trading activity. This may be done to predict future price changes. In order to forecast how prices will move in the future, a technical analyst examines data from the past. They are of the opinion that, when it comes to the stock market, history tends to repeat itself, and that a company's success in the past is the greatest sign of what will happen in the future.

The distinction between these two strategies, whether fundamental or technical, may be boiled down to the question of who is in control of the situation.

The domain of interest for technical analysis is that which is outside the direct influence of an organization. For instance, the price of a stock responds in a consistent manner to the degree to which individuals feel positive over the prospect of a certain stock. When there is a lot of demand for a certain stock, the price of that stock will normally go up. People have a positive outlook on the stock because they believe it offers opportunities for development in the years to come. Regrettably, the qualities of fundamental analysis do not have a direct influence on the level of interest that people have in purchasing a stock or the expectations that they have about the growth potential of the company in the future.

Fundamental analysts rely to earnings reports and other data produced by corporations in order to get this type of insight into the performance of the company. These reports and data offer some indication of how well or badly the company is functioning in some way. The fundamental analyst examines the state of the firm as a whole and attempts to get a comprehensive understanding of how the market responds to the various reports that are released.

On the other hand, the technical analyst is more concerned with the performance of the stock in the past and charts this data in attempt to anticipate the movement of the stock in the future.

This study makes use of a wide range of tools, as well as many distinct kinds of charts, including bar charts, line charts, and candlestick charts. Drawing trend lines through important highs or lows in price movements on a chart helps traders detect things such as the strength or weakness of support or resistance levels. This may be done by identifying where significant highs or lows in price movements have occurred. The most profitable times at which to enter and leave the market may be determined with the use of trend lines.

The actual methods that are used in charting may vary from one technical analysis tool to another; nonetheless, each of these instruments offers a distinctive perspective on the past. Investors may find that using technical analysis to determine whether or not a certain investment is worthwhile for their money is a helpful tool. By analyzing a stock's historical performance, one may get insight into the stock's potential future worth.

For instance, if the historical closing price of a company is $20 per share, and the price of that stock drops to $15 per share, then investors may have some reason to expect that the price will go back up again closer to $20 per share rather than breaking through the support level.

Choosing the Right Crypto Trading Platform

It is essential for any trader, whether experienced or just starting out, to be able to keep up with all of the latest advancements in the market. Additionally, one must choose the appropriate trading platform, which will enable them to monitor the most recent variations in price and keep up with the most recent happenings in the world of cryptocurrencies. Coinbase and Mitrade are just two examples of the kinds of trading platforms that traders like due of this factor.

According to data provided by CoinMarketCap, the following cryptocurrencies now rank in the top ten:

Bitcoin (BTC), Ethereum (ETH), and Ripple (XRP) are all cryptocurrencies.

Bitcoin Cash (BCH), Tether (USDT), and Litecoin (LTC) are three cryptocurrencies.

Binance Coin, abbreviated as BNB

The EOS coin (EOS).

Bitcoin Silver (BTCS)

Bitcoin Cash (BCH)

There should be no charges charged for either deposits or withdrawals on any reputable site. It should also be easy even for interested beginners to set up a new account and should also provide a demo account or version for practice. After all, nobody would risk their money on something that they do not yet have a complete grasp on, so there is no use in trying to convince them otherwise.

How Is It Possible To Generate A Profit When Trading Cryptocurrency?

Gains or losses incurred by trading cryptocurrencies are comparable to those incurred through investing in the stock market in that they exist only on paper until a sell or exchange takes place. Since it has just been ten years since the introduction of the very first Bitcoin to the market, discussing long-term patterns about cryptocurrencies could seem like an exaggeration to some people. However, we are unable to reject the fact that the development of the most prominent cryptocurrencies is extremely good, if not great. This is a reality that cannot be refuted. These days, cryptocurrency traders do not trade as often as they formerly did but rather risk significant portions of their capital on a long-term gain.

Transactions involving Cryptocurrency

When considering the price movement over a short period of time, cryptocurrencies have the potential to become the most volatile of investments due to the rapidity with which fortunes may be created or lost. Even the most well-established cryptocurrencies are subject to the everyday occurrence of substantial price fluctuations in either direction. Even if the price of Bitcoin remained relatively stable the day before, modern-day traders of cryptocurrencies do not find it shocking if they saw the price of Bitcoin go down today.

The dangers

When compared to holding stocks, cryptocurrencies do not have any inherent worth beyond their relative rarity since it is sometimes difficult to mine them and they do have limited quantities, exactly like the situation with Bitcoin. This means that the value of a cryptocurrency cannot be determined by its supply and demand. Trading with them obviously comes with a higher level of risk, but it also has the potential to provide higher gains. In addition to this, some cryptocurrencies are difficult or impossible to regulate, which means that there is a chance that the government of the nation would outlaw it if it is seen to be unmanageable. The United States Securities and Exchange Commission (SEC) has already taken a position on the matter by classifying cryptocurrencies as securities and asserting that the exchanges that facilitate their trading need to be subject to the SEC's laws and regulations. This decision was made as of the present time.

There is also a significant incidence of failure associated with cryptocurrencies, which is shown by the fact that over half of the initial coin offerings that were held in 2017 were unsuccessful. This indicates that the majority of these cryptocurrencies were never brought into existence because they lacked both the financial resources and the community that would have helped them succeed.

Moderating the Risk

Exactly as with other kinds of investments, the risks associated with trading cryptocurrencies may be handled by diversifying one's portfolio. This means that an individual should not put all of their money into a single cryptocurrency. Because of its volatility, novice traders are also encouraged to start cautiously and establish their reputation over time, similar to how dollar-cost averaging in stock trading works to spread out the expense of an investment over time. A technique like this may prevent you from achieving larger profits, but it will also shield you from suffering larger losses.

Keep in mind that the Contract for Differences, often known as CFDs, is a complicated financial product that also comes with a significant risk of incurring monetary loss as a result of the use of leverage. Because of this, anywhere in the neighborhood of ninety percent of investors end up losing money while trading in them.

What Was The First Currency To Be Issued Without A Central Authority?

There have been several civilizations in different parts of the globe that have stubbornly opposed the establishment of centralized monetary systems. The notion of Rai stones on the island of Yap is pretty intriguing. These stones express the idea of a blockchain as well as decentralized money in a manner that is simple to grasp, despite the fact that it is quite difficult to determine which one was the biggest or first. Due to the fact that the islanders did not own a significant quantity of gold, they sculpted enormous round stones out of the local limestone in order to create a kind of money that everyone could use if they so desired. After then, they would function as a kind of money. Theoretically, every resident of the island would have been capable of doing this, but in practice, it evolved into a specialized work that was carried out by a select few. The other islanders chose to trade other goods or services in exchange for the stones. Decentralization meant that the system could be joined by anybody at any time and that everyone participated on an equal footing in terms of their rights.

Nevertheless, if you look at the conditions for anything to be viewed as a decent currency, there remained one major problem: transportation. This was a significant obstacle. Moving these stones from one location to another was a living hell because of how heavy and awkward they were. What is the answer? The inhabitants of the island did not physically move the stones; rather, they hid them in various locations, such as in front of churches, houses, and other buildings, and then transferred ownership of the stones virtually. The locals on the island told everyone else in the community who they had just given one of the Rai stones to, and this allowed the plan to be successful. Suddenly, the stones were not only a terrific way to store wealth and a useful unit of accounting, but they were also a useful mode of conveyance, and this was all accomplished without the stones actually needing to be relocated from one location to another.

The whole population of the island was privy to the information necessary to participate in the decentralized system, thus they all knew who the owner of any given stone was.

When you take a look at blockchain technology and cryptocurrencies, you will quickly realize how similar this idea of the Rai stones truly is; the only difference is that the Rai stones are tangible, whilst cryptocurrencies are digital. The use of a blockchain as an underlying technology is necessary for cryptocurrencies because of this reason. This distributed ledger eliminates the possibility of a double spend since the ownership of each currency on the blockchain can be independently verified by each participant. On Yap, the three functions of a monetary system—access to money, sending and receiving money, and supply of money—were decentralized by making it difficult to produce Rai stones but subsequently simple to move them around (through virtual ownership). Additionally, cryptocurrencies need to find solutions to these problems, and in the next chapter, we will go through these issues in a step-by-step manner.

Capital Needs That Are Constantly Changing

The amount of capital that is required varies depending on the market that is being traded. Day traders and swing traders might start with different amounts of money depending on whether they trade in the stock, FX, or futures markets. The amount of cash required depends on the market in which they trade.

In countries such as the United States of America, a minimum account balance of $25,000 is required in order to participate in day trading of stocks. There is no legally mandated minimum amount required to engage in swing trading of stocks; nonetheless, a swing trader should usually have at least $10,000 in their trading account, and preferably $20,000 if they want to make a living from trading.

There is no legally mandated minimum capital need in order to participate in day trading on the foreign exchange market; nonetheless, it is recommended that traders begin with at least $500, and much better, $1,000 or more. The recommended starting capital for swing trading forex is around $1,500, however the amount should ideally be more. With this amount of funds at your disposal, you will be able to enter at least a couple of transactions one after the other.

Start off with at least $5,000 to $7,500 if you want to day trade futures, but expanding your money is a far better and more effective strategy. The finalization of this contract is contingent upon the aforementioned funds being paid. In day trading, a few of the agreements that you make may demand significantly more cash, although a couple of the agreements that you make, such as miniaturized scale contracts, could require significantly less capital.

You require a deposit of at least $10,000, and most likely $20,000 or more, in order to engage in swing trading using a variety of futures contracts. The amount that must be contributed is determined by the margin requirements of the specific contract that is being traded.

A Meaningful Idea Despite Its Silly Name

The phrase "HODL" is essentially a meme that first appeared in the year 2012. Since that time, not only has it gained traction inside the crypto world, but it has also made its way into other circles. The following is a condensed version of the definition that can be found on Wikipedia:

The phrase "hold" (sometimes spelled as "HODL") is a slang term and Internet meme that is used in the Bitcoin community to refer to the act of keeping the cryptocurrency rather than selling it. Hodl is often written as "HODL." It began with a post that was made in December 2013 on the message board of the Bitcoin Forum by a user who seemed to be under the influence of alcohol and whose post included a mistake in the subject line that read "I AM HODLING." Quartz cited it as one of the most important slang expressions in the culture of Bitcoin in 2017 and defined it as an attitude "to stay invested in bitcoin and not to capitulate in the face of plunging prices."

In essence, it indicates that you should not initiate the sale of an item as soon as you become aware that the asset's worth in terms of fiat currency is decreasing on the market. It is the entire opposite of the trader method in the sense that it does not get caught up in the daily highs and lows of a specific cryptocurrency asset. This is one of the many ways in which it is the complete opposite. The belief that the technology behind cryptocurrencies is on the cusp of ushering in a new era of global prosperity is the primary impetus behind the HODL attitude held by many members of the community of cryptocurrency enthusiasts. A significant number of these people are confident that the fact that they have a working cryptocurrency network is already the greatest prize that they can achieve. It was and still is a matter of ideology; cryptocurrencies represent liberation from the oppressive big brother that is the government and the outmoded banking institutions.

However, the idea of philosophically backing cryptocurrencies does not have much appeal to normal investors because of the way it is implemented. Cryptocurrency investing is a matter of need for them, and likely for individuals in your position as well. When it comes to those investors who are focused on the here and now, the most successful strategy is the one that consistently brings in more cash. Traders, as was previously said, have the potential to make profits, but doing so requires them to invest a lot of time and effort and exposes them to the ongoing threat of making poor choices. You would need to put in the work and maintain a steady level of effort if you wanted to be a trader and follow the movement of the market. As I said before, investing in this scenario implies having an additional job.

The HODL strategy is one approach to avoid this. Basically, it entails making investments in one or more forms of digital currency and holding on to those holdings for the longest amount of time feasible. At the same time, the HODL strategy recommends engaging in infrequent trading in order to first recoup one's initial investment in fiat currency and subsequently make a profit as a result of the aforementioned process.

It is a connection between the two different universes. On the one hand, there is the situation of not having any crypto assets, and on the other hand, there is the state of having crypto investments but continually trading with them. The HODL strategy falls somewhere in between these two approaches. You don't need to be a crypto enthusiast to use the HODL investing technique, but you also don't need to be "that guy" who continuously complains about how cryptocurrencies are a fraud despite the fact that he, she, or any other pronoun has no idea what they are talking about. It is a method through which regular individuals who have some (extra) money to invest may obtain a piece of the action in the cryptocurrency market.

This strategy takes into account the chance of you losing everything and throwing away that money because you went to a casino and made a bad wager (however it does not take into account the likelihood of you having fun or receiving free drinks). The good news is that even if anything like this were to occur with HODL (which has never happened before with any major cryptocurrency), it is hoped that your life would not be completely upended as a result. This investment makes use of money that are easily accessible and offers the owner the possibility that they may earn many times that amount in a matter of only a year or two. Or maybe five or 10 in all. You have to be patient if you want to engage in HODLing.

But most significantly, it satisfies the itch you have to do something with crypto by letting you access the realm of cryptography and allowing you to stop worrying about what you're missing out on. If you are reading this, then you most certainly understand what I am talking about, and it is vital that you acknowledge this fact. This psychological component is required for virtually any degree of intentional success in today's world (I use the term "deliberate" to suggest some process that you were working towards, as opposed to stumbling into success). In today's environment, this component is important for almost any level of success. You can finally make that investment in cryptocurrency that everyone is talking about by using HODL, but you won't have to worry about the possibility of slipping into one of the numerous foxholes that exist in the cryptocurrency sector.

The Differences BetweenCryptocurrencies And Their Local Fiat Counterparts

There are three primary uses for money.

It is necessary to recognise and acknowledge money's role as a medium that may be utilized to trade products and services for other commodities and services.

To serve its purpose as a medium that can hold value and enable the accumulation of wealth, money fundamentally has to meet certain requirements.

The function of money as a unit of account must be fulfilled. According to Ammous (2018), it may be used to measure and compare the worth of various items.

Gold is often regarded as the world's first ever form of currency. Gold and fiat currencies, which are both issued by the central bank, serve as benchmarks for determining the value of cryptocurrencies.

It is important to note that the traditional forms of money, such as gold and fiat money, satisfy all of the requirements necessary to be termed money. It would be more suitable to use cryptocurrencies as the means of trade. The reason for this is that cryptocurrencies may be split up into smaller units and can be sent anywhere in the world.

cited: (Ammous, 2018).

One of the most important advantages of gold is that it is the most well-collateralized type of money. The reason for this is because the means of trade has value, in contrast to bank notes or digital money, which are both produced by financial institutions. Cryptocurrencies are a sort of money that is decentralized, as opposed to fiat currencies, which are entirely centralized since they are created by the central bank in accordance with the laws set down by the government. This is one of the most basic distinctions that can be made between cryptocurrencies and fiat currencies.

The fact that there is no central authority overseeing crypto transactions and a general absence of security measures are likely to blame for the high degree of volatility shown by cryptocurrencies. Therefore, the function of the storage of the value and the function of the unit of account are both destroyed by it.

The price volatility of cryptocurrencies is one of the most

serious problems that are associated with them. As a consequence of this, throughout the value transfer, there are not likely to be any significant shifts or variations in the monetary element (Expert 1, 2018). The bulk of cryptocurrencies are moving toward becoming regulated currencies in the hopes of achieving a price that is more stable and seeing less volatility (Expert 5, 2018). In addition, it has been seen that the majority of cryptocurrencies are following a trend that is moving away from a completely decentralized system and toward a more centralized approach. The participants in this centralized system have the ability to make the most of any potential for advancement. The majority of cryptocurrencies now in circulation move away from a decentralized model and toward a centralized one. They accomplish this in spite of the overwhelming odds. It is possible that the value will decline as a result of this transfer. It is possible for its pricing stability to be reduced as a result of increased centralization and the support given by choices about economic policy. According to Aisen and Veiga (2006), cryptocurrencies have the potential to see enormous growth.

In order to win over political support, the use of cryptocurrencies has to be confined to national borders. According to Expert 6, 2018, this would provide governments with the ability to maintain their financial dominance by providing them with the capacity to regulate the economic parameters. On the other hand, this would be a method that, in the end, would lessen the benefits of cryptocurrencies and would result in a system that would be centralized.

It is not possible for us to assert with certainty that cryptocurrencies are not a potential alternative for the currencies that the state provides. In addition, because of this, the national authorities now have a basis to refer to cryptocurrencies as digital assets rather than currency. It becomes more comparable to gold when done in this manner. The question of whether it should be viewed as an asset or as a kind of money still remains unanswered. It is reasonable to characterize Bitcoin as a digital token that may be traded back and forth between two parties in the course of a transaction.

You may determine the value of this coin by comparing it to fiat money or other national currencies.

You are able to trade it for something that is physically present. It is used in little quantities here and there.

The Federal Reserve is covered in Chapter 5.

Informally, the Federal Reserve System is referred to as "the Fed." The United States Congress established the Federal Reserve in 1913 as the nation's primary banking institution. President Woodrow Wilson gave his signature to the Federal Reserve Act in order to establish a financial and monetary system for the nation that would be more reliable and adaptable. This was done in order to benefit the country as a whole.

This legislation was enacted as a reaction to the string of financial crises that occurred one after the other, and its passage came about as a direct result of those crises. The Federal Reserve has taken on an increasingly diverse range of functions and responsibilities ever since it was established as an institution. It is undeniable that its structure has progressed, and it has become common knowledge that it is necessary for the establishment of a steady economy. Many individuals are likewise of the opinion that the Federal Reserve causes more problems than it solves. Let us have a look at the benefits as well as the drawbacks of the Federal Reserve in this section of the book.

The advantages brought forth by the Federal Reserve

Contributed to the development of a national currency

In the years leading up to the establishment of the Federal Reserve System, the United States of America used a number of distinct varieties of currency. Following this event, there was only one common currency that was to be used across the nation, and this contributed to the economy operating in a more efficient manner.

Improves both the predictability and the level of transparency

The rule-based approach that is utilized in the Federal Reserve's monetary policy serves to increase the predictability as well as the transparency of the actions that are made. This is one of the benefits of the system. This, in turn, helps the Central Bank explain its operations to the general public and helps the market forecast what the Fed may do. It also helps the market prepare for potential Fed moves.

This has a huge impact on the lives of people like low interest rates that would be ideal for debtors rather than creditors. This would make the situation more equitable. The participants in the market would also be aware of the intentions of the Fed, allowing them to act properly and save both time and resources.

A robust and secure monetary system

The Federal Reserve System contributes to the administration of the nation's monetary policy by influencing the circumstances of the credit and money markets in the economy. This is done with the goal of maintaining both price stability and full employment in the economy. In addition to this, it assists in the process of regulating and monitoring financial institutions such as banks and a variety of other financial organizations. This is done to ensure that the nation's financial system will safeguard the legal rights of consumers.

There is representation of financial interests

If there were no such system in place, the nation's banks would represent its best interests, which would not be the optimal choice given that financial institutions tend to be more concerned with the private sector than the public one. In addition, the Federal Reserve would require the banks to conduct an independent audit both from the outside and from inside themselves.

If this system were not in place, all audits would have to be conducted internally, which is a risky practice that may result in corruption.

Contributes to an increase in the legitimacy

The Federal Reserve is able to decrease the motivation to back out of the commitments made in the future by establishing guidelines. It is generally accepted that the central bank would be able to regulate inflation at a manageable level in the absence of any regulations; nonetheless, the bank would be tempted to create more money in order to earn greater revenue for the government.

Contain the danger to the whole system.

The mission of the Federal Reserve is to maintain the nation's financial stability and bring the potential for systemic risk in the nation's financial markets under control. In other words, the Fed strives to keep the economy from collapsing.

Additionally, it contributes to the provision of financial services to the federal government and other organizations in the United States, in addition to a number of other financial institutions located in other countries. In addition to all of this, it assists in the management and operation of the various payment systems around the nation.

The Federal Reserve system has a number of drawbacks.

Invasionary and contrary to the Constitution

There is a school of thought that considers the Federal Reserve System to be antithetical to capitalism. Instead of being managed by private companies, the funds are under the supervision of government agencies. As a result of this, there would be an increase in the size of the government, which is why it has received criticism from a lot of people.

Investing in Bitcoin Comes with a Number of Risks

In May of 2011, the value of a bitcoin had a significant price surge, which was followed by another increase in November of 2013. Despite the fact that bitcoin was never intended to be used as a form of equity investment, several investors have shown interest in the cryptocurrency's market.Bitcoin is essentially a means of exchange that may be utilized in various transactions. However, many do not consider it to be a means of exchange and instead acquire it for the value that it offers as an investment.

Despite this, there are a lot of hazards that come along with using bitcoins since they are decentralized. Several organizations, including the Securities and Exchange Commission (SEC), the Financial Industry Regulatory Authority (FINRA), and the Consumer Financial Protection Bureau (CFPB), have issued several warnings to investors.

Bitcoins have experienced an increase in investments recently, but the notion behind them is still relatively novel. The market continues to be quite volatile. If you compare the investments in virtual currency to more traditional investments, you will see that investing in bitcoin is still a risky endeavor since there is no history or credibility to back it up. This is the case because bitcoin has not been around for very long. The stages of development for these cryptocurrencies are still being worked on. According to Barry Silbert, CEO of Digital Currency Group, this is one of the investments with the "highest-risk, highest-return" potential that may be made. The Digital Currency Group develops and invests in firms that deal with blockchain technology and bitcoin.

The Risk of Regulations

Bitcoin is a competitor to the government-issued money that is currently in circulation. There is a good chance that they will be used in criminal operations, the laundering of illicit funds, the commission of unlawful transactions, or the avoidance of taxes. Because of these factors, it is possible that governments may eventually regulate, limit, or outright prohibit the usage and trading of bitcoins in the future. In 2015, the New York State Department of Financial Services reached a consensus on the laws that apply to businesses and people that deal in or trade cryptocurrency. Any transaction involving the purchase, sale, transfer, or storage of bitcoins is required to keep a record of the clients' identities, have a compliance officer, and have capital reserves. In the event that the total of any transaction exceeds $10,000. This is going to be reported.

Because bitcoin and other virtual currencies are not governed by any appropriate rules, the lifespan, liquidity, and universality of these currencies are being called into doubt.

a threat to security

The vast majority of people who hold bitcoins did not acquire their currencies by participation in mining activities. Bitcoin and other digital currencies are traded by these individuals on prominent online marketplaces known as bitcoin exchanges or cryptocurrency exchanges. These markets are also referred to simply as exchanges.

Because Bitcoin transfers take place in a digital format, the Bitcoin virtual system is susceptible to a wide variety of attacks from cybercriminals and malicious software. Thefts of bitcoins have significantly grown during the last several months. If a hacker is able to get access to the hard disc of a bitcoin owner and compromise it, the hacker will be able to steal bitcoin using the owner's private encryption key and then transfer the stolen bitcoin to another account. Because of this, the owner would suffer the loss of their bitcoins to theft. The owner of the business should keep the secret encryption key on a computer that is not connected to the internet in order to avoid fraud and theft of the business's information. You might also write the addresses down on a piece of paper and store them in a secure location.

A digital currency wallet is where bitcoins are kept safe and secure. There have been instances documented in which con artists and fraudsters have been successful in hacking bitcoin exchanges and subsequently gaining access to the digital wallets of the users of such exchanges. For instance, in 2014 the cryptocurrency exchange Mt. Gox in Japan was the target of a cyberattack, and the perpetrators made off with bitcoins worth tens of millions of dollars. After that, they requested that the individuals who were in charge of the exchange abruptly shut it down.

Transactions that take place on a bitcoin network that include the exchange can never be undone after they have been completed. They are not going to change. There is nothing that can be done. Once you have already submitted the money, a third party will not be able to assist you in getting it back. It is not feasible to obtain the money back in any other way than if the person to whom you gave it decides to reimburse you for it. If you run into an issue at this location, you have very few options available to you. When doing transactions using bitcoin, you need to be very careful and detailed.

Explorer of the Blockchain

A blockchain explorer is a website that, as its name suggests, serves as a repository and public ledger for all transactions that have ever been processed using the Bitcoinblockchain. It is similar to a conventional database in the sense that conventional databases often keep an ongoing list of public key identifiers. The only thing you need to do is click on any one of the numerous public keys, and it will display the time of the transaction, the recipient's public key, the status of the transaction (confirmed or unconfirmed), as well as the amount that was sent. As a first step towards understanding how Bitcoin works, we recommend doing some research on blockchain explorers.

The websites blockchain.com and blockchair.com are two examples of blockchain explorers.

btc.com in addition to blockchain.coinmarketcap.com

Open Book or Ledger

In a previous section, we explained that the data that is maintained in blockchains is composed entirely of records of the transferring of BTCs. This is what is referred to as the public ledger, and it is the primary objective of BTC's use of blockchain technology. The usage of the public ledger functionality that blockchain provides was the driving force for Bitcoin's meteoric ascent to prominence, despite the fact that it has many beneficial qualities in terms of security and openness. To hack into and make changes to the public ledger would not only involve a significant amount of computer and human power, but it would also imply changing the fundamental structure of Bitcoin.

There are nodes

The Bitcoin network is presently comprised of ten thousand nodes that are located in various parts of the globe. Although the majority of them are located in the United States and Europe, they may be found all over the globe. There are four different kinds of nodes, including full, super, mining, and soft nodes. This particular one will be examined in more depth throughout this chapter due to the fact that it carries out responsibilities that are distinct from those of the other three. Soft nodes only store a portion of the blockchain ledger, in contrast to full and super nodes, which maintain copies of the whole distributed ledger. Before installing Bitcoin Core software, a user must first ensure that their computer and bandwidth are capable of handling the demands of participating in the Bitcoin network as a node at any of its three levels: full, super, or soft. Only then may they install Bitcoin Core. If you are interested in carrying out this activity, you must ensure that the software is downloaded from the official Bitcoin website.

Working in mines

The mining nodes make up the fourth and final category of nodes. Mining nodes are responsible for the creation of a new block, and it is because of their participation in the network that fresh bitcoins may be released into circulation. Mining is the process of producing new coins and gaining access to them without having to pay for them. Receiving BTC tokens is the incentive for participating in Bitcoin mining. Miners validate transactions while simultaneously seeking the same reward as everyone else. The term for this is "Proof of Work." They are used in two different capacities by the BTC network.

According to Nakamoto, the process of mining Bitcoin is more difficult with each passing year; thus, miners are awarded a decreasing percentage of the total cryptocurrency produced compared to 2009. Checking the Bitcoin Clock is the best way to get an accurate picture of the current BTC supply on the market.

How does one go about mining? In order for a computer to successfully mine Bitcoin, it first has to solve a hash problem, which is an algorithm. In the beginning, when Bitcoin was originally introduced, anybody who had access to a computer could mine Bitcoin. However, as of right now, it is anticipated that there will be new Bitcoins flowing every ten minutes, and there are millions of machines working together to solve hash issues. These issues get more difficult to solve per 2,000 users. At this point in time, the very first thing that one would have to do if they wanted to begin mining Bitcoin is to make the first financial investment in computer power, in addition to purchasing the appropriate mining software.

What exactly is an issue with the hash? It is a tournament consisting of mathematical problems that can only be solved by using a computer. The computer works its way through each possible answer in a competition against other miners to complete the task first and earn you that Bitcoin. It is a competition amongst millions of people. Because of this, in the early days of Bitcoin, it was common to hear statements such as "Oh yeah, they were hacking computers sharing the same network to have them mine BTC." The creation of a one-man mining pool occurs as a result of this process of acquiring more computers.

Coins and Tokens Distributed Through an Initial Coin Offering

The following are the three primary functions that coins and tokens that have been issued during an ICO may fulfil:

They are the end result of the work done by the organisation. They are a means of exchange that may be used for a predetermined quantity of a variety of goods or services. In addition to that, you may trade projects with them.

They denote the entitlement to a profit-sharing arrangement. Coins may be distributed to shareholders in the same manner as traditional shares by the corporation.

They are the end result of the work done by the organisation. Coins are a kind of currency that may be exchanged for a certain quantity of a variety of goods and services. In addition to this, they may be used as a medium for trading in a project.

They represent rights to a share of the profits. Coins, just like traditional shares, may be split up into parts according to a certain proportion.

They represent bonds issued by a corporation. Coins are capable of performing the same functions as loans. The rate at which the owner may accrue interest has been determined in advance.

The Drawbacks of Investing in Initial Coin Offerings

Despite their apparent benefits, initial coin offerings (ICOs) are not without their fair share of drawbacks. To begin, there is a "white paper" that outlines the idea of the new company. There is no indication that any work was done. This white paper is the primary source of information that investors depend on. As a result, individuals open themselves up to the risk of being scammed.

People are led to think by these con artists that they would become wealthy if they participate in initial coin offerings (ICOs). However, they do not keep their word or fulfil their commitments. They continue on their journey after they have obtained the money. They do not create any products of any kind.

For instance, the initial coin offering (ICO) for Mycelium was a massive bust for investors. Following the completion of the fundraising, the members of the team just vanished. After some time had passed, it was eventually found out that they had spent the money on a trip.

One other drawback of initial coin offerings is the fact that some respectable businesses do not possess the necessary technological assistance and/or expertise. They could have the aim of making things, but they do not have the skills or experience to create a successful blockchain firm.

Take CoinDash as an example; it was a complete loss for its investors. Hackers were successful in gaining access to the company's website, which resulted in the loss of many millions of dollars. The hackers changed the address of the ICO wallet to one of their own choosing.

How to Put Your Money Into an ICO

If, despite being aware of the risks associated with investing in an ICO, you are still interested in participating in this endeavour, the following are some things you should bear in mind before doing so:

Always be sure to complete your homework.

It is essential for every company's success to have a current awareness of the most recent industry developments and news. Having said that, this is of utmost significance for investing in ICOs. You are aware that initial coin offerings (ICOs) are companies that need money to expand. Their hypotheses cannot be tested in the real world because they lack funding. As a result, you need to be very careful and thorough in your study. Put the internet to good use for yourself and educate yourself as much as you can about cryptocurrency and initial coin offerings (ICOs).

Determine whether or not the team is capable of delivering. Before approaching the team members and the founders, make sure you have read the white paper in its entirety. Make use of the Internet to learn more about various topics. You may, for instance, discover more about them by using the website LinkedIn. Look at what they have said about themselves on their profiles to get a better idea of their trustworthiness.

Carry out some research on the team, and find out whether or not the individuals have any previous experience working with cryptocurrencies, projects, or ICOs. Acquire as much information as you can, particularly about their participation. If you believe that they are capable of giving you the outcomes that you desire, then you may continue doing more research.

When doing your study, use caution and thoroughness. Investigate them thoroughly to see whether or not they are just con artists or actual fraudsters.

You may sign up for a forum or a group with others who share your interests. You have the option of reading the posts they've made or asking them questions.

Take into consideration the perspectives of seasoned investors.

Ask yourself whether their ideas really accomplish anything to fix the issues or if there is any truth to what they are saying. Think about whether or not their ideas are aimed at a possible market and have the potential to lead to success. Inquire inside yourself what values their initiatives have the potential to deliver to society. Are these individuals proposing new ideas, or are they only repeating something that has already been conceived? Think about the responses. Do not make an investment until you are absolutely certain that the group can do the tasks at a higher level.

Find out what can be done with the tokens.

Initial coin offerings result in the production of brand new tokens for a project. Every project ought to clearly articulate the purpose of the tokens. For instance, you may inquire as to why Ethereum or Bitcoin are insufficient to fulfil the role of tokens for the project.

Determine the amount of money that is being acquired.

In the past, some initial coin offerings (ICOs) were allowed to raise a limitless amount of money. Investors were provided with open caps, which enabled them to contribute an infinite amount of money to various initiatives. In general, the less distinctive the tokens are as currency when traded, the more coins there are in circulation.

In addition to this, you need to find out how the team spends the money and how much of their budget goes towards marketing and how much goes towards product development. Make sure you don't forget to ask how much money they put aside for the critical allocations. Keep in mind that a successful initial coin offering (ICO) is transparent and explains to investors where their money will be spent.

Learn the value of the token.
How much do you think each token is worth right now? As an investor, one of your primary concerns is whether or not the value of your coins will increase over the next several years. You are also interested in finding out if there is a possibility that the market may become oversaturated with such tokens. You are also interested in learning more about the incentives that are associated with these tokens. After all, the only way for

you to make a profit is if the value of your tokens increases.

Discover the process for obtaining tokens and the timetable for doing so.

If the members of the team are covetous, then more than half of the tokens will be allocated in an illegitimate manner. Because of this, you need to have information on how and when the tokens will be allocated. It is important for successful companies to connect the distribution of their tokens to their roadmaps, since each milestone demands a different amount of cash.

Make sure that you also keep an eye on the stage at the time when tokens are being given. There are certain projects that will not distribute tokens until the initial coin offering has concluded. On the other hand, some projects are required to have beta versions before they may begin distributing tokens. However, despite the fact that gaining knowledge about these topics is beneficial, you should not let that information influence your choice to make an investment.

Are you able to make a profit?

My GPU is drawing just over 175 watts to compute at a hash rate of around 53.5 MH/s (mega hashes per second), yet my rig is only averaging 51.4 MH/s in the pool using the approach I've outlined here (with some simple overclocking and GPU optimisation). My daily earnings have been averaging out to around 0.00248 Ether when I mine at this pace. Is there a profit in doing so? Visit whattomine.com and input the model number of your GPU, your cost of power, and the average hash rate of your rig in order to get a decent indication of how unprofitable a single GPU setup is. Keep in mind that you need to amortise the cost of your computer as part of your calculations for how much money you will make mining cryptocurrency.

When I last ran the whole calculation, which was on Christmas Eve in the year

2020, it needed a rig that was capable of around 16,000 MH/s in order to mine one ETH every day. If you wanted to achieve that performance, you would need dozens, if not hundreds, of GPUs that were superior than the one I was using. It is not difficult to establish a mining enterprise for amusement purposes. Developing a successful company by using various tools is a completely other endeavour. Around the world, there are dozens of businesses dedicated to the process of mining cryptocurrencies. It is a realm that you need to educate yourself about very thoroughly.

What exactly is encryption, then?

Encryption is the process of encoding information with the use of algorithms with the intention of prohibiting access to that information by others who are not authorised to see it. The symmetric key technique and the public key method are both common types of encryption that are used for digital communication.

The name "symmetric" comes from the need that both the sender and the receiver have the same key in order for the encryption method to be considered "symmetric."

The encryption key for public key encryption is made accessible to the whole public, however the decryption key can only be accessed by the party that is the intended recipient of the message.

How is it Possible for There to Be Something Called a "Public" Encryption Key?

Utilising a mathematical problem known as prime factorization, often referred to as integer factorization, is one of the most common and widely used methods for generating public encryption keys. Begin with two rather big prime numbers as your starting point. (Some quick maths from the sixth grade As a reminder, a prime number is only capable of being divided by 1 and by itself.) Let's refer to them as P1 and P2, shall we? The outcome of multiplying them together is a composite number, which we will refer to as "C."

(P 1 x P 2 = C)

The value C is an extremely unusual number that has very unique characteristics. It is referred to as a semiprime number since it can only be divided by one, the number itself, and the two prime elements that contributed to it. Because of its unique quality, the number may be used as a public key for encryption purposes.

You are going to utilise C as the public key, and you are going to preserve P1 and P2 as the pair of private keys. Although it is not difficult to produce C, factoring a number that is sufficiently big and has been produced with care might require hundreds, thousands, millions, billions, or even trillions of attempts, depending on the size of the number. Although there are mathematical procedures that may speed up the process, factoring prime numbers in practise must be done by trial and error.

Exchanges For Virtual Currencies

It is recommended that before you start investing in cryptocurrencies, you first have an understanding of how cryptocurrency exchanges function and which specific platforms you may deal with.

Exchanges for Cryptocurrencies: What Exactly Are They?

Since cryptocurrencies are digital currencies, the exchanges where they are exchanged in are digital platforms, websites, which enable transactions such as buying, selling, or trading of cryptocurrencies. A cryptocurrency exchange operates in a manner that is strikingly similar to that of a conventional stock or forex market. Selftrading is an option, professional brokers are easily accessible, and there are tools at your disposal that will assist you in making the most out of each transaction.

These exchange platforms are required to conduct identity verification on its users in order to comply with the regulations governing online transactions. You will need to register a user account on the platform of your choosing, just as you do with social network accounts, email accounts, and other similar accounts. After that, you will be required to validate this account by submitting a government-issued photo identity card to the website.

Even while the vast majority of exchanges demand that users have their accounts verified, you may still discover some that are not too stringent with their requirements. The ability to handle self-made, straight-forward deals is something that all of these different exchanges have in common.

The Many Forms That Exchanges ForCryptocurrencies Can Take

There are several cryptocurrencies accessible, and investors and traders in digital assets may choose from a variety of exchanges to buy, sell, or trade their holdings. If you are interested in entering the world of cryptocurrencies, the following information will provide you with an introduction to the three key exchanges that you should think about using.

1. Traders and Brokers

When dealing with brokers, you are dealing with websites that have been created solely for the aim of selling bitcoins. The pricing is determined by the website of the broker. A cryptocurrency broker might be compared to a store that also provides services related to currency exchange.

2. Market Places and Exchanges

The trading platforms for cryptocurrencies accomplish their purpose by bringing together vendors and buyers in a single location. The sites generate revenue by deducting a predetermined amount from each and every transaction that is carried out inside the portal. One may refer to this as the service cost that they charge. Trading platforms provide for wonderful channels for trading that is uncomplicated and quick.

3. Markets for Direct Transactions

Direct trading systems are distinct from standard bitcoin trading platforms in that they are able to facilitate more complicated deals on the platform itself. Participants in the system are able to participate in genuine dynamic trades, in addition to the system's primary function of serving as a marketplace for buying and selling bitcoins.

In addition, the platform enables investors from all around the globe to engage in ongoing trading, in addition to buying and selling of cryptocurrencies. Traders are not restricted by predetermined market prices for their cryptocurrencies, in contrast to the case with regular platforms. They have the ability to determine the pricing for these digital assets on their own. The decision of whether or not to go through with an exchange now lies solely in the hands of the other investors.

As can be seen, there is a wide variety of exchanges for cryptocurrencies, ranging from the most simple to the most complicated. You may anticipate that, as an investor, you will be required to travel through all of these channels in order to participate in the transaction.

What Qualities Should You Search for in a Cryptocurrency Trading Platform?

It is important that you do not just choose the first investment opportunity that you come across, just as it is imperative that you do not choose the first investment channel that you come across. In this scenario, you will be working with digital assets that have actual monetary values attached to them. Because of this, you shouldn't leave anything to the luck of the draw. Before you even think of purchasing cryptocurrencies in order to trade with them, you need do some research first since the internet is home to many different exchanges.

If you are unsure how to get started, the following tips are offered in the hopes that they may be of assistance to you throughout your quest for the most appropriate exchange.

• A sense of veracity

When it comes to trading cryptocurrencies, credibility is of the utmost importance. You do not want to risk having your money go to waste or dealing with complications that are not essential just because you did not research your selected exchange.

You have the Internet on your side; make the most of it by using it to your advantage. In addition to investigating the platform in question, look for evaluations written by users who have really put the platform to good use and achieved positive results. Another great choice is to inquire about potential references. Additionally, reliable websites pertaining to the sector might be examined as an additional resource. You may also engage in forums if you want more help in this matter.

• The Procedures and Prerequisites for Signing Up

When it comes to setting up a new account, you should prioritise ease of use above all else. You wish to establish a trading account in a matter of minutes and then complete the verification process in an equivalently brief length of time. Your selected exchange has to be optimised to the point where it has an effective integrated registration system, which is especially important given that you are operating in the digital sphere.

Imagine how troublesome the platform may be when it comes to the actual transaction interface if your exchange is unable to even polish the registration procedure. In addition to this, it is essential to have actual verification techniques. The majority of the time, cryptocurrency exchanges that are unable to verify accounts in a timely manner do so because they lack the appropriate technologies. In this scenario, there is a good likelihood that they do not possess the appropriate technology for the service or the security.

• Authentication and Safety Measures

Although verification is necessary, the identity criteria should not be too burdensome or impossible to meet. In most cases, all that is required to transfer money into or out of your account is an identification card issued by the government in your country. The verification process might take as little as a few minutes or as long as several days, but be assured that it will keep both your account and your transactions safe at all times.

You will be able to discover exchanges that will provide you the ability to transact in the system while maintaining your anonymity. These are the interactions that you need to keep a close eye out for. In most cases, they provide just a limited amount of protection or encryption, both of which may easily put your transactions, not to mention your trading account on the platform, in jeopardy. When it comes to anything of this kind, it is strongly recommended that you complete the whole verification procedure. Defend yourself from cybercriminals and con artists.

• Circumstances or Limitations Inherent in the Geography

The trading of cryptocurrencies is subject to the same kinds of rules and restrictions that govern forex trading. As a consequence of this, the capabilities of the site may vary from one region to another. It's possible that there are some tools that are available to you in one nation but not in another. It is for this reason that you should look for an exchange that is totally consistent with the geographical rules of your nation.

• Currency Trade Rates

When it comes to currency conversion rates, you'll notice that they might vary from one site to the next. When looking for places to trade cryptocurrencies, you should adopt the mentality of "shopping around" because of this very reason. There are occasions when an exchange will provide rates that are noticeably lower than the rate that is currently available on the market. You could also get fortunate and obtain favourable exchange rates that work to your advantage. This would be a win-win situation. Spend some time evaluating different rates and services in order to choose the exchange platform that offers the greatest overall package for your needs.

• Costs Related to Transactions and Services

You are in possession of several pieces of information that should not be kept secret by means of exchanges. When you pay the page a visit, you should check for the service and transaction prices that they are required to post there since it is mandatory for them to do so.

The costs associated with this often vary from one exchange to another. They are often contingent on the breadth of services that are included in the price of your membership. If you are participating in a straightforward buying and selling exchange platform, as opposed to one that provides constant trading, you may anticipate receiving cheaper rates.

The maxim that "better service comes at a higher price" does not always hold true in this scenario. Because of this, you should not base your selection only on this factor. Find a reputable exchange that can cater to your requirements and provide the services you want at a price that is affordable on your list of priorities in order to succeed in your endeavour.

• Varieties and Procedures of Financial Transactions

Keep in mind that there is actual money involved with cryptocurrencies. If you do want to invest in these digital assets, you will need to give some thought to how you will make payments and how you will get returns. Find information on the payment methods while you are evaluating various exchanges to consider, since this will help you make an informed decision.

There are certain exchanges that allow transactions using credit cards, debit cards, or both. Some may include making direct payments into a bank account. Others will use wire transfers, while others will use more time-efficient methods like PayPal and other online payment systems. You will encounter both types of people while dealing with others.

It is essential that you choose a trading platform that provides customers with as many payment alternatives as is humanly feasible. Keep in mind that you will be doing business with other users of the site, and there is no way to know in advance which payment methods those other users will accept. Your ability to transact inside that system will be simplified according to the number of different payment methods that can be supported by the platform.

Transaction times are directly proportional to the number of different payment methods available. For instance, transactions made using credit cards are safe while at the same time being simpler to verify; as a result, these transactions may be completed in a matter of minutes. When it comes to wire transfers, on the other hand, this kind of transaction requires the manual processing of banks and may take anywhere from several days to even weeks to complete.

A Ten-Day Interval Encompassed Within The Blue Vertical Line.

You can see how the demand zone developed straight from the surge, precisely as it did when the news was released, and this makes for a wonderful back test trade. When seen from this angle, it is very evident that the institutions are at work as a result of the imbalance that occurred with the pricing. The game of patience is also extremely important because you have to wait for either of the zones to obtain a mitigation, and if one of the zones gets mitigated first, you have to search for the entry requirements before you take the trade and set the SL and TP, both of which are very important.

You need to learn to accept whatever the market provides you at any given moment in time and on any given day. The market will not always go from the supply zone to the demand zone for TP, but you must learn to take whatever the market gives you. Because proper trade management is essential, you should never be greedy and always be content with the profit you make.

EXAMPLE OF A CHART NO. 14: A PERIOD OF TEN DAYS CONTAINED WITHIN THE BLUE VERTICAL LINE.

The same thing, it's easy and it works: you just need to be able to recognise and draw the zones, and you'll be ready to go.

Based on the previous example, we won't be looking for chances to purchase on the support either. Because this is an institutional zone, our primary objective is merely the supply zone; have a look at how successful the delivery was; they mitigated the zone twice; possibly profits would have been generated on the first move, which is sufficient.

An Overview Of Virtual Or Online Currencies As Money

Cryptocurrencies, sometimes known as virtual currencies, are a kind of digital medium of exchange that may be created and used by people or groups acting independently. Because the majority of cryptocurrencies are not regulated by national governments, they are seen as alternative currencies and mediums of financial exchange that operate outside the parameters of state monetary policy. This is due to the fact that national governments do not regulate cryptocurrencies.

Bitcoin is the most well-known cryptocurrency and was the first of its kind to gain widespread usage. On the other hand, there are hundreds of different cryptocurrencies, and more are popping up every month.

BTC Mining: A Limited Supply of Resources

Even while mining generates new cryptocurrency units on a regular basis, most cryptocurrencies are intended to have a fixed supply. This is because mining is a resource-intensive process. This generally indicates that, as time goes on, miners will get a decreasing number of new units every new block chain. In the end, the only compensation that miners get for their work is the transaction fee.

This has not yet occurred with any of the existing cryptocurrencies, but experts predict that the last Bitcoin unit will be mined some time in the middle of the 22nd century if the patterns that have been seen so far continue. Therefore, cryptocurrencies with a finite supply of units are more comparable to precious metals like gold than they are to fiat currencies, which potentially have an endless supply of units available.

CRYPTOCURRENCY MARKETPLACES & MARKETS

Many of the most widely used cryptocurrencies can only be traded between users on a peer-to-peer basis in a private transaction. This means that they are not very liquid and may be difficult to value in comparison to other currencies, both crypto and fiat.

Popular cryptocurrencies like Bitcoin and Ripple trade on specialised secondary markets that are comparable to forex exchanges. These markets allow traders to trade cryptocurrencies for fiat currencies. (An example of this is the defunct cryptocurrency exchange Mt. Gox.) These platforms provide users the ability to trade their cryptocurrency holdings for major fiat currencies, such as the United States dollar and the euro, as well as other cryptocurrencies (including less popular cryptocurrencies). They provide their services in exchange for a tiny fee, which is typically less than one percent of the value of each transaction.

Exchanges for cryptocurrencies play an important part in both the formation of liquid markets for popular cryptocurrencies and the determination of their values in comparison to that of traditional currencies. Despite this, pricing on the exchange may still be quite unpredictable.

Make Strategic Use Of Several Time Periods.

Trading off of the 5-minute chart is comparable to operating a vehicle while under the influence of alcohol. You may be able to make it home, but sooner or later, this behaviour will catch up with you.

Trading on low time frames may be enjoyable given the opportunity to see quick price swings. In addition to this, we have the opportunity to compose an entry that is flawless. Having said that, the quality of the signals that we get at such a low time frame is not very good at all. Why is it the case?

When it comes to traditional charting, the basic guideline is that the stronger the signal, the longer the time period should be. This is because the price action, when seen over a longer period of time, is less subject to the fluctuations caused by intra-day trading and is instead more of a function of the fundamental trend.

Think about different time periods as if you were a scientist examining something under a microscope. You need to play about with the magnification until things start making sense, being acquainted with each time frame, and being able to comprehend each signal in its own unique context.

This begs the question, doesn't it? How can we determine the appropriate time period to use?

Moving up to a greater time period is your best choice if you discover that you are having difficulty appropriately interpreting the signals in the market. If necessary, the 4-hour chart should be changed to a 12-hour one, and daily updates should be switched to weekly ones. You should make an effort to zoom out and take in the wider picture rather than focusing on the details of the situation. When the price is at a crucial support or resistance level, you may switch to a lower time period after you've established the fundamental trend and determined whether it will continue.

As you travel around the different time frames, one thing to keep in mind is to be cautious not to keep changing them to explain your directional bias. This is an important consideration. You need to be consistent in the way that you approach trade inspection in order to avoid making this error. When coming up with trade ideas, a consistent time period should be used.

"You can look at any time frame, but just as a general rule, the longer the time frame, the stronger the signal."

The craze that is CryptoKitties

The game CryptoKitties is powered by blockchain technology and allows users to purchase, trade, and breed digital cats. It was developed by the Canadian business Axiom Zen, which has its headquarters in Vancouver. The debut of CryptoKitties in November 2017 contributed to the rise in popularity of the game.

Decentralised apps (DApps) may be created using non-fungible tokens (NFTs), and CryptoKitties is a great example of this. It is one of the first games to employ blockchain technology, and it serves as the finest illustration of how this technology can be used to produce something that is pleasant and enjoyable for the general audience.

The primary objective of CryptoKitties is to breed uncommon cats that can be sold for a high price on the open market. You begin the game with two cats, which you may subsequently use to mate with one another in the hopes of producing unique offspring.

The popularity of CryptoKitties may be attributed to a number of factors. The fact that it is enjoyable to play is by far the most significant of them, however. It is an interactive game in which you may construct new virtual cats, each of which has its own characteristics and qualities. Because of this, it's not simply a game anymore. It provides a chance for artistic expression in addition to being an instrument for financial gain.

If you're just getting started in the world of cryptocurrencies, you may be curious about how CryptoKitties operate.

How does the CryptoKitties platform function?

The functionality of CryptoKitties is based on the use of smart contracts that are hosted on the Ethereumblockchain. This indicates that the people who own the Kitties are the exclusive proprietors of the animals, and no one else does. You are free to purchase, sell, and even breed your cats on the market; no one will try to stop you from doing any of these things. There is no centralised authority that is in charge of the transactions, yet they are all recorded on the blockchain anyway.

In addition to this, every single Kitty has its own individual set of distinguishing qualities or attributes. When a new Kitty is formed on the blockchain platform, all of these characteristics, including colour, pattern, eyes colour, and coat pattern, are generated at random. These characteristics include: colour, pattern, eyes colour, and coat pattern. During breeding sessions, these characteristics may be handed on from parent to offspring, leading to the development of new characteristics and novel combinations.

On the blockchain, each of these characteristics as well as their values are recorded. This ensures that they cannot have their integrity compromised or be altered in any manner. Also, due to the fact that the owners of the kittens are the ones who own them, there is no governing body that has the power to decide to take them away from you.

Where Can CryptoKitties Be Purchased?

If you are interested in purchasing a CryptoKitty, the first thing you need to do is sign up for an account on the site itself. After you have completed this step, you will be able to go to the marketplace and buy a Kitty from one of the vendors that are located there. After that, a private key will be generated for you that will let you to access your Kitty that is stored on the blockchain.

This particular private key is exclusive to your account and may only be used with the Kitty that you own. Therefore, even if a third party has access to it, they won't be able to use it to get access to your Kitty even if they have their very own similar account! This indicates that there is no possibility for anybody other than yourself to get possession of your Kitty without first obtaining your authorization.

What is the current value of a CryptoKitties?

When CryptoKitties were originally introduced to the market, the price of one of these digital collectibles was a fraction of what it is now. In the beginning, they were only valued roughly $10 apiece, which made them easily available to any and all those who want to get one. The value of CryptoKitties has also significantly grown as more and more individuals are becoming connected with the cryptocurrency on a daily basis.

One CryptoKitty is now valued anything from $100 to $20,000, depending on market conditions. The worth of these things is only going to go up in the coming years as a result of the growing number of individuals who are interested in them. Therefore, if you have been considering participating in the CryptoKitties community, right now would be the ideal moment to do so!

Your data might be revealed to others who you never intended to see it if something were to happen, however with blockchain technology, this would be impossible because:

Data is encrypted using the technology behind cryptocurrencies, so all that others will see is a series of numbers. There will be no names, addresses, or other information that may be used to track you down.

Because there is no centralised database and everything is decentralised, nobody will be able to sell your information for a profit or provide it to another person without either your knowledge or your permission.

Blockchain technology offers a solution to a multitude of issues that are present in all other current financial systems, most notably the issue of trust.

When a transaction takes place, such as when someone transfers another person some cryptocurrency (bitcoin or any other kind), the transaction is instantly broadcast, and every node gets an updated version of it automatically.

However, in order for a blockchain network to accept any kind of transaction, there are two things that need to be verified first: authorisation and authentication.

Authentication: It is necessary to provide proof that you are who you claim to be in order to establish ownership.

Authorization: Additionally, there has to be verification that you are able to carry out the tasks that you are attempting to carry out.

This private key cryptography technique is made available by the blockchain system, which makes it simple to ascertain the aforementioned two aspects.

People on the blockchain network who possess cryptocurrencies are each assigned a private key, which serves as an indication that the holder of the key has a certain quantity of that coin.

It is this private key that is used to validate the authorisation and authentication of users. So, instead of writing a cheque to someone and having the bank call your house to verify if you actually wrote the cheque or having them go through your account to determine if you have enough money to afford that transaction, a straightforward set of numbers is used to confirm authorization and authentication on the blockchain network. This is analogous to what would happen if you wrote a cheque to someone and had the bank call your house to verify if you actually wrote the cheque.

Therefore, blockchain technology provides a means by which any internet user can transfer digital property (not just cryptocurrency) to another in a way that is safe, secure, and guaranteed. This ensures that everyone is aware that the transaction has taken place, and that no one can successfully claim that the transfer is invalid. Blockchaintechnology is not limited to cryptocurrencies.

Maintaining the Safety of Your Cryptocurrency

Over the course of the last year, there has been a rise in interest in cryptocurrencies among the general public, as well as among the media, the financial sector, and investors. This has resulted in a surge in value that is unparalleled for all of the most prominent cryptocurrencies. When it broke beyond the $4,500 threshold in 2017, the price of one Bitcoin reached a new all-time high. At this time, the cost of both Ether and Dash has surpassed the level of $350. The values of several other prominent cryptocurrencies are continuously going up in price. Because of their great worth, it should come as no surprise that dishonest individuals may attempt to steal your cryptocurrency. As bitcoin gains in popularity and acceptance, there is a commensurate increase in the number of storage choices that are now becoming accessible. This is a cause for optimism. However, since there is such a vast variety of alternatives to choose from when it comes to digital wallets, picking the best one may be difficult, especially for someone who is just starting out. When it comes to most types of digital wallets, making the best decision involves finding a happy medium between ease of use and safety.

There are two factors that you need to take into consideration while selecting the most suitable bitcoin wallet for your requirements. These two terms refer to the value of the transaction and the volume of the transactions. The number of cryptocurrency coins that are sent or received in a transaction is referred to as the transaction's "transaction value." The number of times you buy, sell, or exchange cryptocurrencies in a certain amount of time is referred to as transaction volume. It is essential to keep in mind that the values described here are simply relative and will differ from one individual to the next. On the other hand, these factors are of critical significance while selecting the appropriate digital wallet.

In the next section, we will take a look at the many kinds of bitcoin wallets, as well as the ways in which the transaction value and the transaction volume influence each option.

Wallets available online

These are quite easy to use and provide a great deal of convenience in addition to their ease of usage. People who conduct a modest number and value of transactions are suitable candidates for using online wallets. Basically, if you just want to keep relatively little quantities of cryptocurrencies and do not plan to make numerous transactions, online wallets could be a viable alternative for you. This is because online wallets are more secure than traditional paper wallets. The fact that you may access them from any location—provided that you have internet connection—contributes to the ease with which they can be used. They can be accessed with only an email account and a password, so the learning curve for using them is rather low. Due to the fact that they may be accessed from any place, they do not provide the highest level of security. This is a drawback. Utilising a password that is very difficult to crack is one of the best ways to ensure the safety of your online wallet.

Wallets on mobile devices

Mobile wallets are not only straightforward to use but also provide the highest possible level of convenience. People who often deal in bitcoin transactions of little value should strongly consider using them as an alternative. If, for example, you use cryptocurrencies on a regular basis to pay for access to online gaming platforms or to pay for housing while on vacation, the most suitable solution for you is a mobile wallet since it allows you to store and access bitcoin on the go. The fact that most individuals constantly have their cellphones with them makes mobile wallets a very handy payment option. In this manner, you will have an easier time paying for services rendered on the spot. When compared to internet wallets, mobile wallets provide a higher level of security. If you are going to use a mobile wallet, you need to make a note of your seed phrase and save it in a secure location.

Wallets made of paper

Paper wallets provide a good level of protection. Unfortunately, these are the bitcoin wallets with the least amount of convenience. Because of this, they are an excellent choice for those who do a relatively modest number of transactions yet have significant transaction values. To put it another way, if you want to keep a substantial quantity of cryptocurrency coins but do not intend to use them regularly, a paper wallet is the option that you should go with. Avoid using an internet provider to create your paper wallet if you want the highest possible level of safety. If it's at all feasible, you should make your own paper wallet.

Wallets Made of Hardware

These digital currency wallets provide the highest level of protection available. In addition to this, they provide a great deal of convenience. As a result of this, they are an excellent option for those who often engage in bitcoin transactions of a considerable value. One may easily mistake a USB flash drive for a hardware wallet at first glance. On the other hand, these flash drives are equipped with a specialised chip that stores the private key to your bitcoin wallet rather than the standard storage space found in other flash drives. Even if someone breaks into your computer and steals your personal information, your digital wallet will still be safe because of this.

Before you are allowed access to the private key stored on a hardware wallet, you are also required to provide a password. Even if your wallet is stolen, you won't lose any money because of this protection. It is extremely recommended that you write down your seed and save the information in a secure location, just as it is with other types of wallets. Because of this, you will still be able to access your cryptocurrency money even in the event that you misplace your hardware wallet. Hardware wallets, in contrast to the other solutions for bitcoin wallets, do not come at no cost. To purchase one, there will be a cost involved on your part.

NXT is widely regarded as one of the most innovative cryptocurrencies currently in circulation. NXT was first conceived of as a "second generation cryptocurrency" by an unknown programmer in the year 2013. NXT, in contrast to many other prominent cryptocurrencies, was not constructed using the codebase that was supplied by Bitcoin or Ethereum; rather, it was constructed using Java from the bottom up. As a result, it was able to differentiate itself from other cryptocurrencies in some respects while preserving certain connections with them.

The fundamental notion behind NXT was that it would take fundamental ideas and concepts from Bitcoin and

Ethereum and expand upon them in order to provide a fully functional blockchain platform that could be put to use for almost any purpose. The amount of available tokens is a significant point of difference between NXT and Bitcoin. The proof-of-work protocol, often known as mining, is continuously responsible for the generation of new bitcoins. However, the NXT economy has a fixed amount of money, which implies that mining cannot produce further currencies and hence does not exist in this environment. Rather, proof of stake, which refers to the ownership of NXT tokens by an individual, is used to verify transactions. In point of fact, "proof of stake" may be considered as a proof of concept for the NXT cryptocurrency. This is because 100% proof-of-stake blockchains were previously believed to be impossible to implement.

Using proof-of-stake implies that anybody may verify a block using any device, even something as basic as a Raspberry Pi or a smartphone. This opens up the possibility of decentralised verification of transactions. There is no such thing as specialised gear designed for "NXT mining," and even very minor players still have a possibility of verifying a block and earning a reward for their efforts.

Proof of stake consensus algorithms are inherently more efficient than proof of work consensus algorithms. This means that transactions will be completed at a quicker rate compared to what they would be using Bitcoin or even Litecoin.

To design a platform that could incorporate many distinct vital blockchain capabilities inside a single blockchain was another major notion that was central to the project. As a result of this, NXT is not just a cryptocurrency for transferring money; it also offers a suite of services, including additional currencies, an asset exchange for share trading, data storage, a messaging system, an alias registration system, and even a voting module that can be useful in any setting, whether it be political or business. Users are able to simply add their own features to the NXT client and develop new applications thanks to its extensive support for a variety of plugins. In addition, it offers a broad array of support for these plugins.

It is possible that the support that the NXT system provides for new monetary systems is the most striking aspect of it. The newly formed currencies have the NXT currency's backing, but operate independently of the NXT coin itself. According to the unnamed creator of NXT, BCNext, it is recommended that the cryptocurrency known as NXT not be regarded as the most essential currency of the system but rather as the basis for the creation of brand new currencies.

NXT currency and Bitcoin are digital assets with very different applications. The NXT currency is not intended to be a key feature in and of itself; rather, it is intended to function as a component of a platform that is far larger. In the meanwhile, the main reason why the blockchain technology behind Bitcoin was developed was to create a digital money that could really be used. In the meanwhile, platforms like as NXT and Ethereum both enable the development of new cryptocurrencies in addition to new services on top of their respective blockchains.

When everything was said and done, the goal of the NXT project was to develop a cryptocurrency of the next generation. In that regard, it was successful, and market capitalization rankings place NXT in the top 20 cryptocurrencies at the present time. NXT is a unique cryptocurrency that is worth keeping an eye on, despite the fact that it is not nearly as well-known or as commonly utilised as Bitcoin and Ethereum.

Where Can I Purchase Bitcoin?

In the past, purchasing Bitcoin was an activity that required a lot of time and was often awkward. The procedure is now much less complicated and difficult, much like the process of converting currency while travelling to a different country.

You have two options when it comes to purchasing Bitcoin. The first is to use fiat cash, such as the United States Dollar, the Euro, or any other major world currency, to purchase Bitcoin via an online exchange. These cryptocurrency exchanges are very much like the traditional currency exchanges that you are probably already familiar with.

Prices are subject to daily fluctuations, and similar to standard currency exchange markets, these ones are open around the clock. These exchanges generate revenue from cryptocurrency transactions by tacking on a minuscule fee to each and every one of those transactions.

On some marketplaces, fees are levied not just on buyers but also on sellers, whilst on others, fees are levied only when customers buy Bitcoin. Before allowing you to make a purchase, the majority of these marketplaces will want to see a valid form of identification from you as an additional safety measure.

Take note of the different kinds of payments that are supported by each of the exchanges. While some exchanges may take payments made through wire transfer or PayPal, others will only accept payments made by debit or credit card.

The trading of

You may use the following three of the most prominent currency exchanges to acquire cryptocurrencies such as Bitcoin, Ethereum, and other altcoins using fiat currencies such as the United States dollar or the British pound. These currency exchanges accept a wide variety of payment methods.

The Coinbase

Coinbase is the most popular cryptocurrency exchange and may be found in countries all over the globe. It gives users the ability to buy, sell, and keep bitcoin in their accounts. Beginners that are interested in trading cryptocurrency almost always use Coinbase as their platform of choice. At the moment, Coinbase enables users to trade cryptocurrencies such as Bitcoin, Ethereum, and LiteCoin using fiat cash as a foundation.

It is well-known for the security measures that it takes and the insurance policies that it maintains on stored currencies. In addition to that, it offers a fully functional software for smartphones that can be used to purchase and sell items while the user is on the go. It is helpful when you want to trade even during your downtime, and you don't need to have your laptop with you all the time. You can do it on your mobile device.

As soon as your registration is complete and your identity has been validated, you will be able to immediately begin acquiring Bitcoin using your debit or credit card.

The Kraken

The headquarters of Kraken are in Canada. It is the most significant marketplace in terms of the amount of purchases made in Euros. This exchange is compatible with a wider variety of coins. It is compatible with Bitcoin as well as Ethereum Classic, Dogecoin, and Monero in addition to Bitcoin. Kraken enables trading on margin, which may not be suitable for novice traders.

You will need to access an exchange that allows trading of cryptocurrencies with other cryptocurrencies in order to trade alternative cryptocurrencies. Poloniex is the most reliable option available in this respect.

The Poloniex

Poloniex is often regarded as the most complete cryptocurrency exchange currently accessible due to the fact that it supports more than one hundred distinct cryptocurrencies and provides data analysis tailored exclusively for expert traders. It offers relatively minimal costs for trading. You won't be able to utilise Poloniex if this is your first time purchasing Bitcoin since the exchange doesn't accept deposits in traditional currencies like dollars or euros. Before you can use Poloniex, you will first need to acquire some Bitcoins using Coinbase or Kraken. After that, you will be able to use Poloniex.

The Basics Of Buying And Selling Bitcoins

It is crucial to understand how to purchase and sell bitcoins in a secure manner, regardless of whether you want to start using them for transactions or whether you plan to start investing and trading with bitcoins.

In order to purchase bitcoins, you would need to:

Look for a Bitcoin Trading Platform That Is Trustworthy: Exchanges for bitcoin are online marketplaces where buyers and sellers of bitcoin may come together to do business. On bitcoin exchanges, it is simple to identify individuals who are willing to sell you bitcoins and accept payment in your native currency. Additionally, you are able to sell your bitcoins in return for local currency on these exchanges.

Coinbase, LocalBitcoins, BITQUICK, BitBargain, Coincorner, and Xapo are some of the bitcoin exchanges that you may pick from. Other options include BitBargain and Coincorner. You are free to experiment on any of these platforms in order to find the solution that best meets your needs.

You need to be able to keep your bitcoins in a safe and secure area where hackers and thieves would not have access in order to own or trade bitcoins, thus you need to choose a storage option. This is a very crucial component of owning or trading bitcoins. Keep in mind that transactions carried out on the network cannot be reversed, which means that you must protect your bitcoins.

There are three primary options available to you for storing your bitcoins:

Wallets Online Bitcoin exchange firms often provide online wallets for their users so that users may securely keep their bitcoins after doing transactions using the platform's services.

To get access to online wallets, all that is required of you is to sign up for an account with any of the bitcoin exchange platforms that were discussed earlier; after that, you will be able to begin utilising the wallets that are provided by those platforms.

You should give Coinbase a try since it is a user-friendly platform that is easy to learn how to use, and it is a decent place to store your cryptocurrency.

Software Wallets: These sorts of wallets come in the form of software that you can download on your computer and then start using it to store your bitcoins. Hardware Wallets: These types of wallets come in the form of physical wallets that you can carry about with you.

You have the option of experimenting with several brands like as Electrum, Exodus, Bitcoin Core, Copay, and Armoury.

Hardware wallets are constructed in the same way as flash drives. You may buy them on the internet and then use them to keep your bitcoins once you have bought them. The Trezor hardware wallet and the Ledger USB wallet are two well-known examples of popular brands of hardware wallets.

Mobile Wallets: Mobile wallets are digital wallets that may be downloaded into mobile devices, such as smartphones and tablets, and then carried with the user at all times for use in completing financial transactions. Mycelium, Xapo, Blockchain, and Bitcoin wallet are just a few examples of well-known bitcoin mobile wallets that you may test out.

Begin the Process of a Transaction: After you have finished setting up your wallet, the next step is to go ahead and buy some bitcoins for your account. To begin, you will be required to sign up for an account on the exchange and link your bank account to it. This will allow the exchange to deduct the cost of any coins that you buy from your bank account, and when you sell bitcoins, your bank account will be credited with the amount of local currency that is comparable to the amount of bitcoins that you sold.

You will need to visit the area of the exchange website labelled "sell bitcoins" in order to define the worth of bitcoins you intend to purchase and the rate at which you are ready to acquire them. This step may or may not be required, depending on the trading platform you choose.

The exchange will automatically pair you up with another user who is also looking to sell their bitcoins at the same time. After you have completed the payment, the whole amount of the coins you have purchased will be deposited into your bitcoin wallet.

If you want to sell your bitcoins, you will need to go through the same procedure as before. First, you will need to begin a transaction, then you will need to transfer the coins to the buyer, and finally, your local bank account will be credited with the amount of money that is comparable to the amount of bitcoins that you sold.

E-book readers are, in my opinion, the primary reason why people switch from reading physical books (p-books) to reading electronic books (e-books). Exactly for this reason, I decided to build a collection of e-books. Calibre provides complete support for an extensive selection of e-book readers. Over 40 different e-book readers are presently supported by calibre in their entirety. Yes, I'm far over 40. Everything from e-readers like the Kindle, Kobo, and Nook to mobile phones and tablets is included in this category.

5.1: Loading an electronic book onto your electronic book reader

Establish a connection between your electronic book reader and your computer, and launch calibre if it isn't already open. The 'Device' symbol will display next to the 'Library' button in the tool bar if calibre is able to recognise your hardware as a compatible device. When you click the 'Device' button, the book list will change from showing the books in your library to showing the e-books that are now stored on your connected device. If you want to transmit an e-book to your device, all you have to do is go back to your library, choose the 'Library' option, and then click the 'transmit to device' button in the top tool bar. It may be summed up in one simple sentence. Another feature that sees regular usage is the capability to delete e-books from the device. To do this, just choose the book you want to delete from the device and then click the "Remove books" option located in the top tool bar.

When you are through managing the e-books that are saved on your device, choose the 'Device' button and then click the down arrow that is located next to the 'Device' button. You should notice an eject icon, which resembles a triangle with its tip facing upward and enclosed in a circle. When you click the eject symbol on your computer, your electronic book reader will be disconnected from the device. Before unplugging your device, you should always eject it first. It is possible that you may regret not doing this in the future.

5.2: Configuration options available for an electronic book reader

Calibrate may be configured to interact with your device in a variety of different ways; however, in this post, I will only discuss the two choices that are most often customised by users.

Click the 'Sending books to devices' button after opening the 'Preferences' menu. In this section, you may modify the save template to alter the location on your device where e-books are stored. You should find this to be extremely familiar if you have any prior experience with music tagging programmes that allow you to establish unique save places. If you have a device such as a Kindle or Kobo, you won't find this to be particularly helpful, and you may safely stick with the settings that came with the device. This is a really helpful feature to have on a device like the Cybook Gen 3 that allows for the organisation of files into folders. Altering the location at which the books are stored may be accomplished via the use of a variety of variables, which are described below the template. Let's take a look at a fundamental example such as "favorites/title – authors." The word "title" will be changed to the name of the book, "authors" will be changed to the name of the book's author, and the book will be saved in the folder labelled "favourites." Under the template field, a full list of all of the possible replacements that may be made in the save template along with explanations of each one is provided.

Disabling supported file types and rearranging them might be another beneficial tweak you can make to the setup. Let's use the Cybook Gen 3 once again as an illustration for this. Click 'Plugins' in the 'Preferences' menu, then go to the 'Device Interface plugins' section, choose the 'Cybook Gen 3 / Opus Device Interface', and then click the 'Customise plugin' button. You will find a list of available e-book formats under the device's setup menu. In this section, you will find the option to deactivate any file types that you do not want transferred to your e-book reader. You are also able to rearrange the format selections. When an e-book is sent to the device in a format that is not supported (or is not checked), the device will automatically convert it to the format that is at the top of the list, thus it is important that this format be checked.

How Companies Can Get Started With The Acceptance Of Bitcoin

The market for cryptocurrencies is now being dominated by bitcoins. They are the most widely used and well known kind of digital money. There are a growing number of major corporations who recognise bitcoin as a legitimate form of currency. This means that customers may pay for the companies' online goods and services using bitcoin. It would be a mistake not to accept these newly discovered online coins as cash given the high probability of transferring and earning Bitcoins. Bitcoin is a decentralised digital currency that can be bought and sold online.

HOW CAN BUSINESSES START TO ACCEPT BITCOIN AS PAYMENT?

1. Establishing your own Bitcoin address.

To begin, you are going to need a Bitcoin wallet. Customers will submit their payments to this address, and the procedure is quite similar to sending an email: they will input your address (or, more likely, scan your QR code with their smartphone), enter the required amount, and then click "Send."

It is quite likely that, just as with a cash register, you will be required to remove the cash at the end of each business day and store it in a secure location. In general, it is a good practise to keep just a modest amount of bitcoin on your computer, mobile device, or server for everyday usage. This is because bitcoin prices may be quite volatile. It is possible that you may prefer to invest the majority of your money in a more secure setting. When it comes to protecting your company's money, it is important that you follow basic best practises.

Using a payment processor When introducing Bitcoin to your company, it is important to locate the most reliable and user-friendly payment processor or the most effective Bitcoin merchant solution that permits Bitcoin acceptance.

Find a partner that can manage the process by allowing you to take Bitcoin payments but instantly converting them into FIAT cash. This will make things easier for you and protect you from the high volatility that is associated with Bitcoin. In this way, your payment will be made in a national currency, and you won't even have to deal directly with Bitcoin at any point throughout the process.

You will find a list of some of the most well-known payment processors in the following paragraphs:

BitKassa is a merchant that accepts Bitcoin as a payment solution.

BtPago is a payment processor that accepts bitcoin in addition to credit cards.

BitPay is a Bitcoin payment processor that also provides a mobile checkout option.

Btbay is a Bitcoin payment processor that also provides a mobile checkout option.

Bitcoin Point of Sale, or BtPOS, is a payment processor that is used in both brick and mortar and online retailers.

Coinbase is a payment processor that provides payment buttons, checkout pages, shopping cart integration, and daily cash outs in USD.

Coinify is a platform that enables users to make Bitcoin Web Payments, Bitcoin Mobile Checkouts, Bitcoin In-store Payments, and Bitcoin Invoices with recurring billing in Bitcoin.

Connected—Full-service banking, payment buttons, internal pages, hardware POS terminals, and credit cards.

Brick-and-mortar hardware POS terminals that also integrate payment processing are available via XBTerminal and GoCoin respectively. GoCoin is an international payment gateway and processing platform for merchants.

Payment processors often demand a charge in the form of a percentage of each transaction or a flat monthly rate in exchange for their services; nevertheless, these costs are far lower than those levied by credit card companies or PayPal.

Additionally, payment processors will provide a few applications of their technology, such as the ability to send electronic invoices, set up a point-of-sale system (which is helpful if, for example, you manage a restaurant or a cafe), or add a shopping cart plug-in to your online store.

Independent Application OfBlockchain Technology

Despite the fact that cryptocurrencies make significant use of blockchain technology, the technology itself has a great many other applications. This does not change the fact that the creation of Bitcoin, which was the first use of this technology in the mainstream, was pushed by Satoshi Nakamoto, a pseudonym given to the person or people credited with creating Bitcoin.

Having said that, ever since the innovation was brought to the attention of the general public, in part because to cryptocurrencies such as Bitcoin and other crypto coins that are based on the Blockchain technology, the technology itself has found various applications, and many multinational organisations and banks are experimenting with its usage.

numerous people are thinking about using Blockchain technology today, in part because of the underlying technology that is offered by a public ledger, which, as we have discussed and seen, is at the core of Blockchain. Blockchain technology has numerous applications in many different areas of business, including commerce, government, healthcare, and basically any area of company that employs a database. Blockchain technology has made it possible to do away with the need for people and companies to place their faith in a third party middleman. Additionally, it has simplified the process of conducting commercial transactions and maintaining records in a manner that was before impossible.

You may be considering entering the competition now that you are aware of this information since you are aware that technology often benefits early adopters and that early users of the internet are now multimillionaires.

Before Making An Investment, It Is Important To Think About The Characteristics Of Cryptocurrencies.

1. The Capitalization of the Market and the Daily Trading Volume

The total value of all coins that are now in circulation is what is referred to as the market capitalization of a cryptocurrency. A high market capitalization may indicate either a high value per coin or just a large supply of coins that are currently available. Perhaps even more significant than market capitalization is the daily trading volume, which can be defined as the total value of the coins that change hands on a daily basis. A robust economy that sees a lot of transactions is indicated by a high daily trading volume in comparison to the market capitalization of the company.

2. The Method of Verification

One of the most important distinctions between cryptocurrencies and traditional currencies is the verification process. The term "proof of work" refers to the most traditional and widespread approach. In order for a computer to earn the privilege of verifying a transaction, it must first spend time and effort finding the solution to a challenging mathematical problem. The problem with this technology is that in order for it to be functional, it needs a significant quantity of energy. Proof-of-take systems are an attempt to solve this problem by delegating the responsibility of verifying transactions to the user who has the biggest portion of the currency. These systems operate with less computing power and claim to have quicker transaction rates, however because of concerns about security, very few can use an entirely proof-of-take-based system. These systems also need less storage space.

3. The Acceptance of Renters

If you are unable to purchase anything with your cryptocurrency, it does not serve much of a purpose. Before you make an investment in a certain currency, you should do your research to find out whether businesses are willing to take it. There are several cryptocurrencies that are widely acknowledged, and some of them even advertise partnerships. has big stores and merchants. Some cryptocurrencies, on the other hand, have a more restricted acceptance, while others may only be traded for other forms of cryptocurrency. Some coins are not intended to be used in transactions involving goods and were instead minted with another purpose in mind.

An Introduction To The History Of Non-Fungible Tokens

Let's go into the past of non-fungible tokens to learn more about their functions and applications, as well as to get a deeper knowledge of how these tokens are employed in commercial transactions. Since the inception of blockchain technology, non-fungible tokens have been used in several contexts. Bitcoin, the very first cryptocurrency ever created, resulted in the production of a digital asset that was completely under the control of its producers. Because of the name given to these assets, which was "bitcoins," their owners were given a heightened sense of significance. A user might have possession of the coins and use them to buy or sell real-world assets (mostly BTC) over the Bitcoin network using the

Bitcoin network. This meant that these assets might be used to produce fiat money on the blockchain, which was something that had never been done before at the time. since of this, early adopters of Bitcoin had an advantage over other people who were interested in purchasing cryptocurrencies since there was an easy method to utilise them to purchase items in the real world. The cryptocurrencyBitcoin inspired the creation of a number of the very first NFT games. Spells of Genesis (SoG) and CryptoKitties are two examples of games that enable it possible to use their respective cryptocurrencies throughout a match.

The years 2017 and 2018 saw the beginning of a considerable expansion in the popularity of NFTs. This was mostly due to the widespread understanding of cryptocurrencies and their application on the blockchain. These games centred primarily on the creation of a digital asset that could be exchanged for fiat currency or other real-world assets. However, a growing number of players expressed an interest in learning more about the creation of progressive gaming experiences utilising NFTs and other blockchain-based technologies. That led to the development of CryptoKitties, which shot to prominence almost immediately after its release. By the time 2017 came to a close, it had raised more than 12 million dollars from various investors. That was a major deal at the time, especially for a game that was built on blockchain technology. According to reports, the price of a CryptoKitty was so high that a digital cat sold for a total of $110,000. That indicates that the cost was comparable to that of an original piece of artwork! This demonstrates how helpful NFTs may be in certain situations. They may be used to construct items that not only have worth inside the game but also have relevance in the real world. The ERC-721 prototype wasn't developed until much later, after the enormous success of CryptoKitties. CryptoKitties and the fact that it brought the concept of NFTs to the attention of an even bigger audience are among the primary factors that led to the development of this standard. This demonstrated that those who had never heard of blockchain technology before now had an understanding of what it was, how it functioned, and how it might be used in a game. Around this time, blockchain technology started to become more widespread, which helped raise the number of developers who realised the utility in NFTs and other blockchain tools. Additionally, this helped boost the number of people who used blockchain technology.

Today, non-fungible tokens may be used in any game since it is simple to create them and include them into games. The rise in popularity of NFTs has opened the door to a wide variety of new gaming opportunities that were previously considered to be impossible. It is also important to point out that numerous games are currently being created with the intention of elevating the value of NFTs. According to what we have said before, we consider NFTs to be more useful and versatile than traditional digital assets. For instance, CryptoKitties keeps track of the total number of cats that have been created and even enables users to collect and sell the virtual pets they have created.

In a short amount of time, we will start to see a significant number of games that base their primary currency on non-fungible tokens. Because of this, users will be able to make purchases of items, services, and other types of investments inside the game using NFTs. These assets might be of any kind, from guns to cars and everything in between.

How Can I Make Money By Trading And Staking Cryptocurrency?

If you want to make money by staking, also known as proof-of-stake, you need to already hold a few hundred cryptocurrencies, which you can get at exchanges by buying them with fiat currency. To begin earning a return on what you have invested, all you need in addition to that is a wallet that is dedicated just to stakes. It is also recommended that you use a computer that is solely dedicated to this activity. In order to improve the likelihood of being selected as the fortunate forger at a certain moment, the computer must be let to run for the maximum amount of time allowed.

You need to have a virtual wallet and an account with an exchange before you can begin trading individual units of digital currency. There are websites that provide both options in order to make things simpler for new users.

One website that falls under this category is known as www.coinbase.com. To make your very own wallet, all you need to do is join up for the service. After that, you will need to link your bank account, credit card, or debit card to the website so that you may convert one or two cryptocurrencies into and out of your fiat currency. After you have everything set up, you are free to swap US dollars into other cryptocurrencies, such as Bitcoin, and vice versa.

You may trade cryptocurrencies and fiat currencies in a few different ways: limit trading, market trading, and stop limiting are the three main approaches.

A trader who uses limit trading is able to purchase or sell a group of tokens at a price of his or her choosing. This tactic calls for a lot of forethought on your part. If you want someone to take you up on your offer to purchase or sell anything, then you need to establish a price that is reasonable in light of the fluctuating prices on the market.

When compared to limit trading, the transaction rate in market trading is always guaranteed to be quicker. You are able to purchase or sell at the current market price when you do this. Because they are aware that your proposal is reasonable (at least for the time being), prospective business partners will most likely accept your offer without delay.

Last but not least, stop limitation gives you the ability to activate an order if the price reaches a certain ceiling. For instance, if you set a purchase order for $10, then the instant the price hits $10 or less, it will begin purchasing the item on its own without further intervention from you.

Given the very volatile nature of cryptocurrency markets, do you find that you have any kind of reservations regarding trading? That is very reasonable given the very genuine nature of the threat. In spite of this, there's no reason you shouldn't test the waters and see what it's like, particularly if you're interested in doing so. After all, there are certain benefits to it as well. If you are successful in this endeavour, you will be eligible to receive incentives as a result of that achievement.

Suggestions From The Insider

The following is a list of advice that, if followed, will help you have a more positive experience as a whole and will increase the likelihood of your making a profitable investment.

Never Invest Based on Emotion — When it comes to making financial decisions, you can't rely on how you feel about something since that's not how investing works. You are unable to make an investment in a coin that "feels" good if the price of that coin is really low. Do your homework, find out how successful it has been in the past, and investigate its current tendencies before basing your selection on any of that information.

Invest with Longevity is a principle that applies to all different kinds of financial investments. Investing is not a "get rich quick" technique; rather, it is something that requires patience. When you make an investment in cryptocurrencies, you should plan on keeping your holdings for a significant amount of time. It is not a race; rather, it is a marathon.

Pick Platforms that Have a Solid Reputation When it comes to choosing a platform for your money, there is no better group of individuals to consult for advice than those who are currently using the platform in question. Examine the ratings and results that come from a wide variety of sources on multiple platforms, and choose the ones that are rated the highest. There is no situation that is more disheartening than investing money in something, only to find out later that the platform is terrible.

Be Aware of Fees - This is something that you need to proceed with extreme caution on. There are occasions when there may be an initial offer that gives the impression that it cut the price of the coin, but then it will turn around and charge you a significant amount of money in post-transaction fees. Before you put your money into anything, you should be sure you have a solid understanding of what you're getting into.

Another piece of advice that applies to all types of investing is to not put all of your money into the market. When it comes to depositing money into your fund, you shouldn't put all of your eggs in one basket, and you shouldn't utilise all of the eggs that you have too. In the event that things do not go as planned, it is important to ensure that you have sufficient funds to enable you to stand on your own two feet. Having said that, if you have $200 in your bank account, you shouldn't put more than $195 of it into Bitcoin.

It should go without saying that you should educate yourself, yet a surprising number of individuals still ignore this piece of advice. When it comes to investing in the cryptocurrency market, it is crucial to make sure that you know all there is to know about the coin that you are looking at. This is because there is a lot of information out there. Always be aware of what is happening in the market, and look for ways to adapt to it.Determining What Cryptocurrency Is in Chapter 1

Cryptocurrencies are an innovative and fascinating new financial system that has quickly become a widespread phenomenon. A cryptocurrency is an innovative kind of digital money that also represents a brand-new form of technology that was developed in response to a breakthrough in the field of computer science. To have a firm grasp on all there is to know about cryptocurrencies, the fundamental ideas behind them must first be comprehended. In this chapter, we will investigate the components that go into creating a cryptocurrency. We are going to take a look at the criteria that must be completed before we can call anything a cryptocurrency. We will also educate ourselves on blockchain, the underlying technology that underpins cryptocurrency. In the last part of this discussion, we will investigate the function of cryptography in the protection of cryptocurrencies.

According to the work of a researcher called Jan Lansky who is affiliated with the University of Finance and Administration in Prague, a cryptocurrency is described as a system that satisfies six specific characteristics. To begin, it can't have any dependence on a single governing body. Additionally, it is required to maintain an exhaustive record of the currency units as well as the owners of those units. A cryptocurrency must describe when new currency units may be generated, as well as the mechanism by which new units are created and held. Additionally, the cryptocurrency must explain the procedure by which existing currency units can be traded. Each unit of money is required to have a proof of ownership, which is done via the use of cryptography. Transactions that result in a change of ownership of cryptocurrency units have to be compatible with the cryptocurrency system. Last but not least, in the event that there are numerous instructions for transferring ownership of the same unit, it is only possible to carry out one of those instructions. These requirements serve as a guide for developing and establishing a cryptocurrency, much in the same way as the laws of physics that govern robotics do.

By their very design, cryptocurrencies do not have a central administration. According to Lansky's explanation, a cryptocurrency cannot depend on a single, centralised authority source. The decentralised blockchain technology that underpins cryptocurrencies does not need the deployment of a centralised server for conducting transactions or maintaining records. Instead, cryptocurrencies depend on a decentralised network of computers called a peer-to-peer network, in which each participant stores a complete record of the transaction on their own device. The previous attempts at creating digital currencies depended on a third-party company or service, but cryptocurrencies use something that is known as a distributed ledger to record transactions. A distributed ledger is a kind of network that maintains an updated record, in this instance, transactions, across many separate nodes, which are also known as users.

A cryptocurrency is required to preserve a full record of every unit, including details such as the identity of the owner of each unit. This is shown by the transaction data that is stored on the blockchain. You are aware of the location of every cryptocurrency unit as well as the person who owns it if you are familiar with the transaction history of every digital wallet that is used to store bitcoin. For instance, the transaction history of a wallet address may show that it has received 5 bitcoins and has sent out 3 bitcoins. Without having to explicitly access the data stored in the wallet, we may deduce from this information that the wallet contains a total of 2 bitcoins. The blockchain technology that underpins cryptocurrency saves all of the transaction data in a format that can be read but cannot realistically be changed. This is only possible because of the cryptographic time stamp.

In order for a system to be recognised as a cryptocurrency, it is necessary for it to describe, in a straightforward manner, how new units of money are generated and who receives them. When users validate transaction data by generating cryptographic hashes, new cryptocoin units are generated in the case of Bitcoin. This process is called mining. The activity referred to here is mining. Computers that participate in the mining process and successfully verify encrypted transaction data are rewarded with additional units of crypt currencies. This is done as a kind of incentive. This is the method through which fresh Bitcoins are introduced into circulation and made available for purchase. This is analogous to the process through which natural resources, once extracted, are converted into cash.

Transactions that alter the ownership of the units need to be able to take place if a cryptocurrency system is to function properly. This is something that is fundamental to both the blockchain and Bitcoin. When using a Bitcoin client, it is possible to send and receive bitcoin units across different addresses. The network that also issues the statements proving ownership of cryptocurrency units also issues the statements for these types of transactions. For instance, you might transmit 20 Bitcoins from your address to another, and the network would keep track of both the transaction and who now owns the cryptocoins. This would be possible because the network is decentralised. It is necessary for a cryptocurrency to first satisfy this requirement before it can be deemed to be one.

Last but not least, there has to be a prerequisite for activities to be carried out concurrently as desired. There is a possibility that the system would be confronted with the need to deliver the same quantity of bitcoin to many destinations at the same time. Given the circumstances, it is imperative that at least one of the commands be satisfied. If this criterion is not met, orders that are entered at the same time cannot be completed. When it comes to Bitcoin, if two orders are filed at the same time for changing the ownership of one unit of bitcoin, at least one order gets completed. This is because Bitcoin is a proof-of-work system. By doing so, we eliminate the possibility of fraud and duplicate expenditure. This last criterion is a safeguard against inappropriate use of the coin.

These are the six essential requirements for a cryptocurrency to function properly. If a system is capable of fulfilling all of these characteristics, then it has the potential to function as a cryptocurrency. A cryptocurrency is always a digital currency, but a digital currency is not always a cryptocurrency. However, a digital currency is always a cryptocurrency. In summary: decentralised, a full record of units, an explanation of the method by which new units are created and ownership is transferred, ownership can be proven by transactions, and there is a solution for when several transactions are conducted simultaneously on the same unit. A system is only considered to be a cryptocurrency if and when all of these conditions are met. Bitcoin, the first cryptocurrency, will serve as a blueprint for constructing these needs. Bitcoin is often cited as the first cryptocurrency ever created, and this is certainly not a stretch of the imagination.